A Life with CARNIVOROUS PLANTS

VICTOR ROOK

Copyright © 2024 Rook Communications. All rights reserved. No part of this publication may be used or reproduced in any manner whatsoever without written permission from the publisher, except in the case of brief quotations embodied in critical articles and reviews.

ISBN: 978-0-9766653-2-8

Photographs by Victor Rook with a few from Wikipedia Commons (Public Domain), Shutterstock & Pixabay.com.

Author website: victorrook.com

ROOK COMMUNICATIONS PUBLISHING

Cover photo: Back hood of a *Sarracenia* 'Judith Hindle'

Dedicated to Mom

TABLE OF CONTENTS

INTRODUCTION 1
  My Story 1
  History of Carnivorous Plants 3
    Discoveries 3
    Habitats of Carnivorous Plants 4
    Species of Carnivorous Plants 5
    Conclusion 6
  Movies & TV with Man-Eating Plants 7
    Movies 7
    TV Shows 10
SUPPLIES 11
  Plants 11
    Big-Box Stores 12
    Carnivorous Plant Nurseries and Online 13
    Community Growers 14
  Containers 14
    Pots 15
    Saucers 15
    Trays and Bins 16
    Terrariums 17
    Bog Gardens 18

Soil	19
GROWING	**21**
Potting	21
Repotting	22
Water	23
Distilled Water	23
Rainwater	24
Reverse Osmosis	25
Going on Vacation	25
Light	26
Outdoors	26
Indoors	28
Dormancy	30
Refrigerator Method	30
Outdoors	32
Propagation	34
Pests & Diseases	34
VENUS FLYTRAPS	**35**
Overview	35
Growing	36
Feeding	37
Dormancy	39
Propagating	40
Division	40
Seeds	42
Cuttings	44
Gallery	46
PITCHER PLANTS	**61**
Overview	61
Growing	64
Feeding	66
Dormancy	67
Propagating	69
Division	69

- Seeds 70
    - Hybridization 74
    - Cuttings 76
  - Gallery 78
- SUNDEWS 93
  - Overview 93
  - Growing 94
  - Feeding 97
  - Dormancy 99
  - Propagating 99
    - Seeds 100
    - Division 101
    - Cuttings 101
  - Gallery 102
- BUTTERWORTS 111
  - Overview 111
  - Growing 113
  - Feeding 116
  - Dormancy 117
  - Propagating 118
    - Seeds 119
    - Division 120
    - Cuttings 120
  - Gallery 122
- CONCLUSION 129
  - Videos 131
  - Your Support 132
- RESOURCES 133
  - Plant Suppliers 133
  - Lighting & More 134
  - Social Media 135
    - Facebook Groups 135
    - YouTube Channels 136
    - Instagram 136

INTRODUCTION

MY STORY

It's about 1973-74, and we've just moved into our third apartment on Oakland Avenue in Medina, New York. My mother continues to support me and my two siblings while waitressing at the local restaurants. I had developed a love of houseplants a year prior when I received a bean-growing science kit as a birthday gift. It consisted of a "magic" bean, a Petri dish with some sort of sticky growing substrate, and a clear plastic cone to contain the moisture. It wasn't long before that bean sprouted and wound its green tentacles around the poles of my upright desk. I was transfixed.

Soon after I discovered Muchow's Floral Shop, which was a couple of miles away. It would be the first nursery I would visit, and as the years went by, I frequented it often. They even sold some of my macramé plant hangers—yet another hobby I'd begin in my youth.

Muchow's was full of aisles of lush plants that ran from the entry floral shop area to the farthest ends of the greenhouses. Smaller potted plants were the first to greet you, and if you turned the corner, a room full of large plants—*Monsteras* (Swiss Cheese Plants), *Scheffleras* (Umbrella Trees),

A LIFE WITH CARNIVOROUS PLANTS

Dieffenbachias (Dumb Canes), *Sansevierias* (Snake Plants) and more made you feel as if you were in a tropical jungle. After saving up my allowance, I would later purchase my first *Monstera* there. But that's a story for another day. I left it out on the sunny balcony one day and all the beautiful leaves burned to a crisp. I was heartbroken.

On one of my visits, I recall seeing these odd plants known as Venus flytraps. They would snap shut when you touched them, and they ate bugs! I don't remember how much they cost at the time—I'm thinking around $3—but I begged my mother to get them for me. A week or so later she placed two she had purchased after work on the kitchen table. It felt like having alien creatures in the house. I was mesmerized and fascinated. How grateful I am to this day that she bought those for me.

Well, as most kids do, I made a lot of mistakes in raising them. I knew they needed lots of water, but I probably watered them from the tap. I knew they needed a lot of sunlight, but I probably kept them inside their humidity domes, which is a great way to cook plants in the afternoon sun. And I probably fussed over getting a fly inside a trap with a pair of tweezers. I didn't just leave them be. I needed a performance. I needed to see them kill and eat!

I can still remember the two plants sitting in trays by my bedroom window. No matter how hard I tried, I just couldn't keep them alive, and they slowly faded away.

INTRODUCTION

Me at Oakland Ave. in Medina, NY.

I would say they lived for a few months. Looking back and what I know now, it was most likely the mineralized tap water that did them in. Naturally, I was sad for my loss. But I would try again several times years later.

In this book you'll see what I've learned to keep your Venus flytraps—and other carnivorous plants—alive and healthy for years and years. You'll even learn how to grow your collection from seeds and other forms of propagation. First, let's get to a little history lesson.

HISTORY OF CARNIVOROUS PLANTS

Carnivorous plants have long captivated the imagination of naturalists, botanists, and curious minds alike. Their peculiar ability to lure, capture, and digest small prey sets them apart from typical vegetation, making them a subject of fascination and study for centuries. In this exploration of carnivorous plants, we delve into their rich history, discover their diverse habitats, and unveil some of the most intriguing species that have evolved over millions of years.

Discoveries

Charles Darwin, the renowned naturalist and author of *On the Origin of Species*, made significant contributions to the

A LIFE WITH CARNIVOROUS PLANTS

study of carnivorous plants. In his book *Insectivorous Plants*, published in 1875, Darwin explores the fascinating world of these botanical predators. He conducted numerous experiments and observations to unravel the mysteries of how carnivorous plants captured and digested their prey. His meticulous research shed light on the mechanisms behind their carnivorous behavior, including the movement of the Venus flytrap's snapping traps and the secretion of digestive enzymes in sundews. Darwin's work not only expanded our understanding of these plants but also highlighted the importance of adaptation and natural selection in the plant kingdom. Here are a few pages from that book.

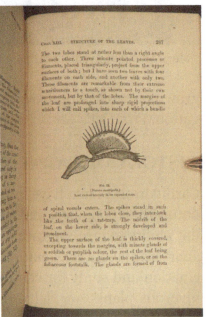

Habitats of Carnivorous Plants

Carnivorous plants are found in a variety of habitats around the world, each of which presents unique challenges and opportunities for these remarkable organisms. They have evolved to thrive in environments where nutrient-poor soils

INTRODUCTION

and limited access to essential nutrients, such as nitrogen and phosphorus, are common. Some of the most prominent habitats for carnivorous plants include:

Bogs and Peatlands: Many carnivorous plants, such as the North American pitcher plants (*Sarracenia* spp.) and sundews (*Drosera* spp.), are adapted to acidic, nutrient-poor peat bogs. These waterlogged environments provide an ideal setting for these plants to capture insects and other small organisms to supplement their nutrient requirements.

Sandy Soils: The coastal plains of the southeastern United States are home to several species of carnivorous plants, including the Venus flytrap (*Dionaea muscipula*). These plants inhabit nutrient-poor sandy soils, where they capture prey to compensate for the lack of nutrients in the ground.

Rainforests: In tropical rainforests, pitcher plants like *Nepenthes* spp. thrive. These plants use modified leaves that form pitcher-like structures to trap insects, and they often grow in nutrient-poor rainforest soils, where they can access additional nutrients through carnivory.

Mountainous Regions: Some carnivorous plants, such as the purple pitcher plant (*Sarracenia purpurea*), can be found in mountainous regions with cold, nutrient-poor soils. These plants have adapted to survive in harsh alpine environments.

Species of Carnivorous Plants

Carnivorous plants encompass a wide range of species, each with their unique adaptations and strategies for capturing prey. Here are a few notable examples:

Venus Flytrap (*Dionaea muscipula*): Native to North and South Carolina in the United States, the Venus flytrap is perhaps the most famous carnivorous plant. It has specialized leaves with hinged traps that snap shut when triggered by a wandering insect, ensnaring and digesting its prey.

Pitcher Plants (*Nepenthes* spp. and *Sarracenia* spp.): Found in various regions worldwide, pitcher plants are known for their distinctive pitcher-shaped leaves. These leaves contain a pool of digestive fluid that attracts, traps, and digests insects.

Sundews (*Drosera* spp.): Sundews are known for their glandular, hair-like structures that secrete a sticky substance to ensnare insects. Once caught, the leaves curl around the prey, facilitating digestion.

Butterworts (*Pinguicula* spp.): Butterworts are small, rosette-forming carnivorous plants that produce sticky leaves to capture and digest insects. They are found in a variety of habitats, including bogs and sandy soils.

Bladderworts (*Utricularia* spp.): These aquatic or semi-aquatic carnivorous plants have small bladder-like structures that rapidly capture tiny aquatic organisms. Bladderworts are incredibly efficient hunters and are found in freshwater habitats worldwide.

Waterwheel Plant (*Aldrovanda vesiculosa*): The waterwheel plant is a free-floating aquatic carnivorous plant with snap-traps that resemble those of the Venus flytrap. It captures aquatic invertebrates and small aquatic organisms as they brush against its traps.

Conclusion

The history of carnivorous plants is a fascinating journey through centuries of discovery, observation, and scientific investigation. From the earliest mentions by ancient philosophers to the meticulous studies of modern botanists, these captivating plants continue to intrigue and inspire. Their ability to thrive in nutrient-poor habitats by supplementing

INTRODUCTION

their diet with insects and other small prey exemplifies the remarkable adaptability and diversity of life on Earth. As our understanding of carnivorous plants continues to evolve, we gain new insights into the complex and wondrous world of nature's ingenious creations.

MOVIES & TV WITH MAN-EATING PLANTS

Here are just a few of the many movies and TV shows that feature carnivorous or "man-eating" plants. Who knows, something like these may really exist out there. Nature *always* finds a way to survive.

Movies

Tarzan's Desert Mystery (1943) - Tarzan, played by Johnny Weissmuller, has a brief encounter with a man-eating plant before he heads off to the desert.

The Land Unknown (1957) - A group of explorers becomes trapped in a prehistoric world hidden within Antarctica. They encounter various prehistoric creatures, including a menacing man-eating plant with tentacles.

Voodoo Island (1957) - A group of researchers and scientists travels to a remote island to investigate mysterious deaths. They discover that the island is home to a voodoo cult and a variety of deadly threats, including man-eating plants.

The Woman Eater (1959) - A deranged scientist finds a carnivorous tree in South America and captures women to feed the deadly plant, which in turn gives him a serum that helps him bring the dead back to life.

A LIFE WITH CARNIVOROUS PLANTS

The Lost World (1960) - In this adaptation of Sir Arthur Conan Doyle's novel, there are grasping plant tentacles, lily pad-like people eaters, and a carnivorous tree with strangling vines.

The Little Shop of Horrors (1960) - This black comedy-horror film features a man-eating plant named Audrey Jr.

Konga (1961) - A British botanist finds a way to grow plants to a very large size. One of the main characters has her arm trapped by a bad plant.

The Day of the Triffids (1963) - This British science fiction film is based on John Wyndham's novel and features mobile, venomous plants that attack humans.

The Navy vs. the Night Monsters (1966) - In this science fiction horror film, a strange plant specimen from an Antarctic expedition grows out of control and attacks the crew of a remote Navy base.

Venus Flytrap (Revenge of Dr. X) (1970) - A mad scientist uses thunder and lightning to turn carnivorous plants into man-eating creatures.

INTRODUCTION

The Mutations (1974) - A botanist combines DNA from plants and people and creates a man-plant with a Venus flytrap chest. Great opening segment on carnivorous plants.

At the Earth's Core (1976) - Explorers discover a subterranean world inhabited by various creatures. Among them is a carnivorous plant with long, snake-like vines and a large mouth that attacks two of the characters during a struggle.

Creepshow (1982) - In "The Lonesome Death of Jordy Verrill," a meteorite causes a man to become enshrouded with debilitating vegetation. *Creepshow 2* (1987) - Animated sequence has Billy luring his bullies to giant Venus flytraps.

Little Shop of Horrors (1986) - A musical comedy-horror film based on the 1960 original, featuring the iconic man-eating plant, Audrey II.

The Crawlers (1993) - Nuclear waste in a small town creates mutant tree roots that entwine and strangle the locals.

Jumanji (1995) - The board game unleashes a variety of dangers, including a gigantic man-eating plant with tentacle vines and a large flower-like mouth to feed.

Journey to the Center of the Earth (2008) - Brendan Fraser and his nephew meet some very large Venus flytraps.

The Ruins (2008) - Carnivorous vines try to ensnare friends in their tendrils, forcing the group to fight for survival.

Dinosaur Island (2014) - A teenage boy and girl are teleported through time and space to an island with dinosaurs and giant man-eating pitcher plants.

A LIFE WITH CARNIVOROUS PLANTS

TV Shows

Doctor Who - In the classic British sci-fi series "Doctor Who," there are carnivorous plants in "The Seeds of Doom" (Season 13, 1976).

The Lost World - In the episode titled "The Guardian" (Season 2, Episode 13, 2001), a plant that looks like a giant succulent demands fresh meat every day or it will emit ammonia gas, thereby holding a tribal village hostage.

The Addams Family - This classic sitcom features a carnivorous plant named "Cleopatra" as part of the family's eccentric household.

Goosebumps - The episode titled "Stay Out of the Basement" (Season 1, Episodes 12-13, 1996) features plant-based horrors when a mad scientist's experiments with plants go awry.

The Simpsons - In episode titled "Moe Baby Blues" (Season 14, Episode 22) Homer's head is eaten by a Venus flytrap at a botanical garden. The same happens to him in "My Fare Lady" (Season 26, Episode 14) in Mr. Burns' office.

SUPPLIES

PLANTS

So you want to get started, but you don't know where to find these incredible plants. There are many places to purchase carnivorous plants, from reputable nurseries to big-box stores. *NEVER* take them from the wild. If you travel to the Carolinas and try to snatch up a Venus flytrap in their native land, you could be facing a felony charge and 25 years in jail. The laws have strengthened since 2014, and I'm glad they have. Efforts are being made to preserve these lands.

The only Venus flytrap we spotted in Green Swamp Preserve, NC.

A LIFE WITH CARNIVOROUS PLANTS

Back in the early '90s, I traveled with a botanist friend to Green Swamp in North Carolina to view Venus flytraps in their habitat. We spotted hundreds of sundew plants with glistening tentacles on the edge of a pond, but we only located one tiny flytrap. Its tall flower stalk gave it away. Poaching was rampant back then. Here are a few more pictures from that trip with my friend Neil.

Sundews (*Drosera intermedia*)

Pitchers (*Sarracenia flava*)

Big-Box Stores

If you've been to Home Depot or Walmart, you may have seen what carnivorous plant enthusiasts like to refer to as "death tubes" or "death cubes." These are pre-packaged individual plants that are grown at nurseries around the country. Unfortunately, as for most plants, big-box stores tend not to provide the proper care to keep them alive. The plants are usually placed on poorly lit shelves among other houseplants. Most dry out and eventually die. If they are moved to a very sunny location, they end up cooking inside their plastic jail. There are

SUPPLIES

thousands of carnivorous plants that never reach their full potential and find a permanent home.

However, I highly recommend that you be vigilant and snatch these up as soon as they become available. That means within a week of them coming off the truck. Carnivorous plants have special needs, and the sooner you can rescue them from certain death, the better. I started my current collection with one Venus flytrap from Walmart and one from Aldi. Within three years those two plants became ten and more with separation and seeds. I'll detail that in the Venus Flytraps chapter.

Carnivorous Plant Nurseries and Online

Pitcher plants, sundews, and butterworts are a little harder to find in your average town. Though a few may end up in those "death cubes," you may have to visit a nursery or order from one that specializes in hard-to-find insectivores. I list several of those places in the Resources chapter.

Try to purchase plants in person if you can. That way you can check for quality and speak to the grower. And what a wonderful way to make a connection with other enthusiasts. Imagine walking through a greenhouse with dozens of *Nepenthes* pitcher plants hanging from baskets and hundreds of Venus flytraps and sundews filling out the raised bins. This would be my version of heaven.

Ordering online may be your only alternative, but it is an excellent option when trying to acquire rarer species. Plants are usually shipped bareroot wrapped in moss. If you order online, be vigilant on when they are expected to arrive and remove them from their packaging as soon as possible. You don't want a box of sundews sitting in a closed mailbox for hours on a 100-degree day. Try to order somewhere close by to reduce shipping miles and stress. Give them time to recover from the "jet-lag" of the trip to your home.

A LIFE WITH CARNIVOROUS PLANTS

Website of Carnivorous Plant Nursery (carnivorousplantnursery.com)

Community Growers

If you live in a populated area, chances are there are people in the community who might be willing to sell or trade carnivorous plants from their own collections. Check out Craigslist, or post in your town Facebook forums. You may find some great deals and make friends in the process. Perhaps even create a club and go on field trips together.

CONTAINERS

Containers are very important when growing carnivorous plants, as you will want to retain the moisture in the soil and provide a relatively humid environment. This could be pots sitting in saucers or trays that you can fill with water, terrariums, or you can even create a bog garden. Here are important factors to consider for each:

SUPPLIES

Pots

First and foremost, if you are keeping your carnivorous plants in plastic pots, only use pots where the bottoms are full of drainage holes. This is so the water can be absorbed up by the soil as the plant needs it. That means no layer of rocks; you want the potting medium to touch the bottom. Press the soil (usually sphagnum peat moss) firmly down.

Saucers

This pitcher plant pot rests in a recycled prepared-salad container. Because the sides of the container are high, this allows it to hold more water at a given time. Pitcher plants have an incredible thirst for water, not only to sustain the plant itself, but also to add to the inside pitcher reservoirs where prey is digested. So take note before you toss out your single-use containers.

To make it easier to provide water to many plants at once, use large plant saucers that you can pick up at Walmart or your garden shop. This way you only have to add water to one container to feed several plants. I have purchased saucers at various sizes to hold a selection of plants in the following collapsible stand.

Trays and Bins

For larger plant collections, invest in trays that you can purchase online or in your store's gardening area. This one keeps my tropical sundews happy during the winter months. It consists of a tray and a clear plastic top with vent slots to allow for airflow. If outside, the top is completely removed.

LeJoy Growing Tray Mini Greenhouse with sliding vents.

Speaking of recycling, the following container once housed a large take-out meal. It even came with vent holes on top.

SUPPLIES

I've made it a container of choice to start Venus flytrap seedlings under indoor plant lights, but it can also serve as a tray for multiple pots.

Terrariums

Some tropical carnivorous plants adapt well to terrarium life, and they look spectacular when grouped with a mix of carnivorous species in their own little world. But BEWARE. Never place a closed terrarium in direct sunlight. The temperature will quickly rise inside and cook your plants. Terrariums also have other inherent problems, like overgrowth, which can lead to crowding, and mold from lack of airflow.

When choosing a terrarium, I prefer a glass container with a wide opening. This allows for airflow and a means for bugs to get to the plants. I also recommend only placing terrariums indoors under plant lights to keep the inside from overheating. Keeping a terrarium outside, even with a wide opening, is too risky.

Stick with tropical carnivorous plants for terrariums, like cape sundews (*Drosera capensis*), Mexican butterworts, and small *Nepenthes* pitcher plants. Keep the soil damp with distilled or rainwater (we will talk more about water later) but be careful not to overwater. The soil should be moist but not saturated.

This container comes with a lid that I slightly crack open for airflow.

Bog Gardens

Temperate insectivores like Venus flytraps, *Sarracenia* pitcher plants, and threadleaf sundews (*Drosera filiformis*) make the perfect outside bog gardens since they all require dormancy. Find a large bowl pot with many holes on the bottom (or drill some) and plant your temperates together. Sit that pot in a deep saucer of water that you keep filled up to the edge.

SUPPLIES

SOIL

Carnivorous plants became carnivorous because they grow in nutrient-deficient soil. That means NEVER use store-bought potting soil, which often contains fertilizers. Use only these ingredients: peat moss, sphagnum moss, perlite, and horticultural sand.

I grow most of my carnivorous plants in peat moss with perlite mixed in for aeration. DO NOT use peat moss or perlite with added fertilizers, like Miracle-Gro®. Live green sphagnum moss is nice on top if you can come by it. Avoid preserved mosses. If you don't mix your own, you can purchase carnivorous plant mixes online. Some growers have worked out special blends that are more suitable for various species. Stick with a general-purpose carnivorous plant mix for your Venus flytraps.

> According to the United States Botanic Garden (usbg.gov): The preferred media for most carnivorous plants are live sphagnum moss, dried long-fiber sphagnum moss, or a mix of about three parts peat moss to one-part clean, sharp sand. *Nepenthes* prefer a more "open" mix, such as long-fiber sphagnum mixed with horticultural charcoal, perlite, vermiculite or other porous aggregate.

If you buy rare carnivorous plants, ask the grower where you've purchased them what soil mixture works best. Dried sphagnum moss is easy to come by at your local garden center. Live sphagnum is not so easy. Check out Etsy.com for live sphagnum moss selections.

Dried from Home Depot.

Live sphagnum from Etsy shop.

Do yourself a favor. Put carnivorous plant soil on your Amazon Wish List. Share the list link with friends & family.

Me receiving carnivorous plant soil on Christmas Day 2021.

GROWING

POTTING

As I noted in the previous chapter, only use sphagnum or peat moss blends specific for carnivorous plants. Always moisten the soil before use. You'll notice that peat moss does not readily absorb water, so you'll want to mix the soil with distilled or rainwater in a bin with your hands before potting it up with your plants. Wring out any excess water before you place it into the pots.

Mix peat moss in a bin with distilled or rainwater.

A LIFE WITH CARNIVOROUS PLANTS

Use pots with drainage holes.

A newly potted *Drosera capensis*.

    You can place a bit of sphagnum moss on the bottom of the pot to cover holes, then add your soil and press down. Remember to only use pots with many holes on the bottom. These are easy to come by as they are the preferred pot of choice used by many houseplant growers. You might even have a few lying around from other plants you've purchased.

    Place the plant into the pot and add soil around the roots up to the green portions of the plant. When potting sundews and butterworts, try to avoid getting any soil or water on the sticky surfaces of the leaves. This can be tricky. Use a small spoon to assist in distributing the soil around the base. Take your time. If soil does get stuck on the leaves, you can knock it off gently with a toothpick, or let it go. New leaves will form eventually as the others die off.

    If you run into mold problems, especially in enclosures like terrariums, sterilize the soil beforehand. Bake soil at 200 degrees Fahrenheit for 1 hour (cover with aluminum foil) and boil dried sphagnum moss in distilled water for five minutes. Strain, cool, and squeeze out excess water.

Repotting

Typically, roots on carnivorous plants grow slowly. So stick with small 3"-4" pots for most single adult plants. It's when they begin to shoot off baby plants that you may want to

GROWING

separate into additional pots, or repot into one that is a bit bigger. In the following picture you can see how crowded the adult Venus flytraps and their offshoots are at the end of a growing season. In early spring I separate out and repot the offshoots. More about propagation in each plant chapter.

WATER

I can't stress enough how important it is to only use distilled, rain, or reverse osmosis water with your carnivorous plant collection. Minerals in tap water can easily kill a carnivorous plant in a few months. They are, indeed, very picky and thirsty drinkers, and should NEVER go dry. Most carnivorous plants require constant moisture in the soil. You should check your plants daily, especially if outdoors. Keep water in the trays they sit in about ½-1" up the sides of the pots.

Distilled Water

Most large grocery stores carry gallon jugs of distilled water. It will say it on the label. Do NOT use spring water or drinking water. I also avoid purified water. I like to recycle those jugs into bird feeders for friends, or keep a few to pour rainwater into.

Cost ranges from $1-$2 a gallon.

Find creative ways to recycle.

Rainwater

A more economical method for providing water for your plants is collecting rainwater, especially if you have enough outdoor space to build a collection system. However, I have found that putting out unused oil drain pans (Dollar Tree) and some pitchers can easily accumulate a half to a gallon or more of rain during a heavy downpour.

Collecting rainwater with a pan.

Using an old-fashioned barrel.

GROWING

Reverse Osmosis

I've heard a lot about this, but never tried it. Beware of water you buy at the store that says "Purified by Reverse Osmosis." That doesn't mean that minerals haven't been added afterward for taste.

Reverse Osmosis (RO) is a water purification process that works on the principle of using a semi-permeable membrane to separate impurities from water. This membrane has very tiny pores that allow water molecules to pass through while blocking larger molecules and contaminants, including minerals. In an RO system, water is pressurized and pushed through the semi-permeable membrane. This pressure is typically achieved using a pump in the system. The pressure is necessary to overcome the natural osmotic pressure, which would normally cause water to flow from the less concentrated side (the clean water side) to the more concentrated side (the impure water side).

Reverse Osmosis systems are available for purchase, but they can become costly and require replacing filters. Most come with water testing kits so you can verify their effectiveness.

Going on Vacation

If you plan on leaving your carnivorous plants for more than two days, here are a few ways to keep them watered.

1. Bring them inside. Water evaporates less quickly indoors. Still, you might want to add a bit more water to the trays and saucers than you normally would.
2. Ask a neighbor or friend to water them. Make sure you choose a trusted and reliable person and tell them to only use the distilled or rainwater you provide for them.

A LIFE WITH CARNIVOROUS PLANTS

3. Create a self-watering system. In the example below, I placed a gallon jug of distilled water in the center of an unused oil drain pan (Dollar Tree) and poked a few holes in it about 1/2" up from the bottom. I made sure the top of the jug had a tight cap on it. Once the water stopped flowing, I placed my Venus flytraps around the edge. As the plants take up the water, the jug will slowly empty. Keeping the cap on the jug prevents all the water from spilling out at once. Do this on a level surface.

LIGHT

Most carnivorous plants need bright light to full sun to achieve their full potential. This is especially true for Venus flytraps and *Sarracenia* pitcher plants. *Nepenthes* and butterworts do best if out of direct sun. Sundews seem to have a range of light intensities that they thrive under. My *Drosera capensis* plants don't tolerate the high summer temperatures as much as my *Drosera filiformis* plants.

Outdoors

Mother Nature knows best, so keeping your carnivorous plants outdoors during growing season is ideal. Not only is bright light freely available, but your plants will also benefit from a constant airflow and an endless supply of bugs to feed

GROWING

on. There is a healing quality when placing your plants outdoors, whether they be carnivorous plants or houseplants. Nature often knows how to tackle things like bug infestations, mold, and disease. Anything that duplicates their natural environment is key to their growth and longevity.

When introducing new plants to outdoor light, it's best to do it slowly. Though they may have originated from outdoors or greenhouse growing conditions, they may also have suffered from low light in a Walmart bin for weeks. Too much light right away can cause leaves to burn.

I like to place my plants outdoors in a shady area first. Then I gradually move them to a sunnier location and block off full sun with a plastic mesh screen. You can buy these at your home improvement store. This cuts down on the intensity of the light. After about 2-3 weeks, I allow them to experience a few hours of direct sunlight. Within a month I remove the mesh completely.

Acclimating a *Sarracenia purpurea* behind a plastic mesh screen.

A LIFE WITH CARNIVOROUS PLANTS

Indoors

If you do not have access to the outdoors in your current living situation, a bright southern-facing windowsill will do for most carnivorous plants. Remember to slowly acclimate your plants to the sun as you would outdoor plants.

If you are unable to receive enough light through your windows, there are some excellent indoor plant lights that you should consider. The key attributes are full spectrum (the colors of the light) and lumens (the intensity of the light). Look for light fixtures that put out full spectrum light with the most lumens you can afford. I have had great success growing sundews and starting Venus flytrap seedlings under full spectrum lamps.

When evaluating indoor plant lights, read the online reviews. You don't want lights that put out too much heat, like metal-halide lights or incandescent bulbs. Look for LED lights, as they tend to be cooler. I prefer a mix of red and blue LEDs to aesthetically mimic natural sunlight.

For my growing rack, I purchased a pair of SZHLUX Grow Light strips for $40 (link in Resources chapter). Each

GROWING

came with chains to hang them from the shelves and metal reflectors to focus the light. They are 40 watts each and have been evaluated at 5440 lumens output. I keep them about 8"-12" away from the tops of the plants and have them on timer for 12 hours a day. The tops of the strips get a little warm, but inside air circulation cools them off.

Grow rack with two SZHLUX light strips.

Search online stores for indoor plant lights that fit your budget. Just keep in mind that they need to put out a lot of light. If less, leave them on for about 16 hours a day.

A LIFE WITH CARNIVOROUS PLANTS

DORMANCY

Like animals, some plants need a good, long rest. This is true for Venus flytraps and *Sarracenia* pitcher plants. We refer to these plants as Temperate. Tropical plants don't require a winter dormancy because there is no real winter in their native habitat. They flourish all year round, though some growth may slow.

Venus flytraps tend to slow down as the light wanes at the end of the summer. As this happens, they begin to slip into dormancy. Allowing flytraps to go into dormancy for the winter months ensures that they will have vigorous new growth the following year. Not allowing flytraps to go dormant—for instance, keeping them inside all year—will eventually kill the plant.

Flytraps need at least three months of temperatures around 40 degrees Fahrenheit. If you live where winter temperatures regularly dip below 20 degrees Fahrenheit, you will want to protect them. Place them on a windowsill in a garage, basement, or in a closed porch that maintains a bit warmer temperature. Reduced light and cooler temperatures trigger temperate carnivorous plants to go dormant.

Dormancy does not mean that you stop watering your plants. You will just have to do it far less often. The soil should remain moist, but not wet, with no excess in saucer.

Refrigerator Method

If you live in the Northern regions where winter temperatures regularly fall into the teens, or a warmer climate, a refrigerator—which maintains a temperature at about 40 degrees—provides a suitable environment for winter dormancy. You'll want to regularly check on your plants to make sure no mold is growing on the soil or leaves. If so, cut off the infected parts and water less.

GROWING

You can also remove the soil from the plant roots, rinse the roots in distilled or rainwater, and place the plant in a plastic bag with damp sphagnum moss around the roots. Personally, I like to keep my plants in their pots. I occasionally cut off dead leaves to allow airflow and prevent mold.

Vegetable drawer with humidity set to medium.

A LIFE WITH CARNIVOROUS PLANTS

Outdoors

As you might have guessed, outdoor dormancy is preferred. Since I live in Virginia where winter temperatures are unpredictable, I have purchased this plastic "cold frame" to protect my flytraps and pitchers from harsh winter winds and temperatures. It has side vents and a zippable top to allow for airflow. If the temperatures dip into the 20s, I cover the enclosure with a thick towel overnight.

Shinegro Mini Greenhouse with PVC tubing and cover.

GROWING

With the outdoor method of dormancy, the plants will still appreciate the light, but growth will cease. Over time leaves will die off. But the plant is not dying. Each species of temperate carnivorous plants has its own telltale signs of dormancy, which I will detail in the plant chapters.

Pitcher plant and Venus flytraps at the end of dormancy.

A LIFE WITH CARNIVOROUS PLANTS

PROPAGATION

All carnivorous plants can be propagated. Some do best with seeds, others with division or leaf cuttings. With a lot of patience and attention, you can quickly double or triple your collection within a few years. I'll detail the best methods for each plant in the following chapters.

Dozens of tiny Venus flytraps growing from seed.

PESTS & DISEASES

Aphids and thrips are known to attack the fleshy growth of several carnivorous plants. Telltale signs are twisted or abnormal leaves. Look closely at your plants and isolate any that have pests or diseases. BioAdvanced 3-in-1 spray is recommended by several advanced growers. Spray only on the non-trap parts of Venus flytraps, pitchers plants, and sundews. Bionide Systemic Insect Control soil granules are also recommended for thrips on pitcher plants. Both are listed in the Resources chapter.

VENUS FLYTRAPS

Jaws of red await,
Innocence hiding sharp teeth,
Flies feel fate's embrace.

OVERVIEW

Because of its incredible ability to quickly snap shut on its prey, the reigning king of all carnivorous plants has to be the Venus flytrap (*Dionaea muscipula*). In the wild it can only be found naturally within about a 70-mile radius of Wilmington, North Carolina.

A set of three trigger hairs on each lobe of the trap send electrical signals to the plant when they are touched more than once within a 2 to 20-second period. Cells on the outsides of the lobes immediately increase in size, forcing the trap to close. If what's inside continues to move, the lobes will close all the way, seal at the edges to form a stomach, and digestive juices will fill the pocket to break down the prey. Depending on the size of the prey, this could take a few days to a couple of weeks.

Once the nutrient-rich juices of the hapless victim have been absorbed by the plant, the trap will reopen to catch more prey. A single trap is usually good for 2-4 meals.

The husk of a fly sticks to a leaf lobe as if the fly were still alive.

As I wrote in the Supplies chapter, it's best to nab Venus flytraps at a big-box store as soon as they become available, visit a nursery that sells them, or order online. To keep your plants alive for years to come, here are their specific growing requirements.

GROWING

1. Venus flytraps need to be kept moist at all times with rain or distilled water. Never use tap water, even if filtered.
2. Venus flytraps should be grown in fertilizer-free milled sphagnum peat moss and perlite. A bit of horticultural sand can also be added, but it is not necessary.
3. Venus flytraps need full sun throughout the growing season. They are, after all, plants, and they do benefit from

photosynthesis. The bright sun gives the lobes their deep red color, which helps attract insects.
4. Venus flytraps need a winter dormancy of about 3-4 months around 40 degrees Fahrenheit.

Refer to the Supplies and Growing chapters for details on purchasing and preparing the soil, obtaining distilled or rainwater, providing adequate light, and dormancy.

FEEDING

Never feed your Venus flytrap meat, as they are incapable of digesting complex proteins. If your plants are kept outdoors during the growing season, you don't need to do anything. Insects are constantly flying and crawling about. Let the plant do what it does best: lure and kill. Trap, wrap, and sap is what I like to call it. A few bugs a month is all a flytrap needs to survive, but you'll see a lot more caught than that.

A leaf reopens to reveal the remains of a spider.

If you keep your flytraps indoors in a sunny location, insects may be hard to come by. Otherwise, you can hand-feed the traps with a pair of tweezers. To slow down an insect's metabolism, place it in a closed container in the freezer for just a few minutes. This may seem cruel, but it prevents you from injuring the insect or leaf by trying to get it into a trap. You can also place the insects and plant inside a closed container for a few hours or overnight until insects are caught. Make sure to keep out of full sun during this time.

Still, my best suggestion is to keep your plants outside where they can feed naturally. Fussing with a plant, whether it be a carnivorous plant or a houseplant, is not good for it. Provide them with what they need in terms of soil, water, and sunlight, and let them be. This also goes for showing off how a trap closes to friends or family. Gather them around and do it once, and that's it. Repeatedly closing traps with your finger or a stick saps valuable energy from the plant.

You may notice that if the trapped prey is too large, or it extends outside of the trap, bacteria may cause the trap to turn black and die. This also happens in nature and is nothing to worry about. New traps will continually replace dead traps throughout the growing season.

Leaves will die off and turn black throughout the season.

VENUS FLYTRAPS

DORMANCY

As discussed in the Growing chapter, Venus flytraps need at least 3-4 months of winter dormancy each year with temperatures around 40 degrees Fahrenheit. They can withstand freezing temperatures for a short period of time, but it's best to protect them from harsh winds and lower temperatures.

Dormancy allows the plant to rest. During dormancy, several leaves will start to die off. Once the leaves turn black, you can cut them off to prevent mold from developing.

PROPAGATING

Venus flytraps can be propagated by rhizome divisions, seeds, and leaf cuttings. Division is by far the quickest and easiest way to increase your flytrap collection.

Division

In October of 2020, I purchased two Venus flytraps. Within three years I've increased this collection fivefold by division.

While your plants are still in dormancy in late winter/early spring, carefully remove them from their pots and separate the rhizomes. They almost fall apart in your hands. There should be a fair number of roots on each.

Now plant them in individual small pots with soil that has been premoistened. Remember to only use unfertilized carnivorous plant soil as described in the Growing chapter.

Return them to where they were kept for dormancy. I like to think of this process as doing it while they are "asleep" so not to disturb the plants. I will sometimes place a few of the plantlets in slightly bigger pots for variation.

Seeds

Venus flytrap flowers rise above the plant in late spring. Flowering takes energy away from trap growth. If you don't want seeds, you can cut the flower stalks off at the base when they are about 2 inches high. This will redirect the energy back to the traps for the growing season.

VENUS FLYTRAPS

If you allow the flowers to be pollinated, seeds will appear a few weeks after the flowers shrivel up. Seeds that are produced by Venus flytrap flowers have a better chance of germinating if they are planted soon after formation. Here is a seed pod ready to be removed.

Place seeds on a paper towel to view them better.

Gently spread the seeds on top of a pot or container of premoistened soil. Do NOT cover them. Venus flytrap seeds need to be on top of the soil to germinate properly. Mist them a bit with distilled or rainwater and set the pot or container in a saucer or tray of distilled water a bit up the base.

Only add water to the base just enough to keep the soil moist but not wet. Cover with a ventilated cover to provide adequate humidity. Place under a bright light or bright but not full sun. I prefer to germinate Venus flytrap seeds under LED lights. After 3-5 weeks you should begin to see baby replicas of adult plants forming. If planted late in the season, you can skip the first dormancy period to give them time to mature.

Separate the traps into pots about a year later if you desire. It will take about three years for the plants to achieve mature plant size and flower. They are very slow growers.

Cuttings

You can also create new plants by *pulling* off a few leaves from mature adults and placing them on top of moistened soil like you would do for seeds. Make sure the pulled white end has contact with the soil. Cut off the trap. Cover with plastic or a clear lid and grow under a light 8-12 inches above the container. About a month later you should see tiny plantlets forming where the pulled tips meet the soil. Allow them to get at least half an inch tall before transplanting.

Make sure pulled tips are under the soil. Wet and cover.

A plantlet forming where the pulled leaf met the soil.

As you can see, there are many ways to significantly increase your Venus flytrap collection in just a few years. For me, division and seeds are the most reliable options. Seedlings take several years to mature into adult plants. Pulled leaves will produce larger plantlets than seedlings.

A LIFE WITH CARNIVOROUS PLANTS

GALLERY

A. Traps at various stages of growth and feeding.
B. This fly had the misfortune of being caught in the teeth of a waiting trap. It freed itself a few hours later.
C. This yellowjacket wasn't so lucky. Enough of its body was lodged inside to convince the trap that it had a meal.
D. By mid-summer there are a lot of hungry mouths to feed.
E. The husk of a mud dauber in its final resting spot.
F. My traps have an affinity for these stinging pests.
G. Phone flashlight reveals the contents within.
H. The pinchers of this earwig were a "dead" giveaway.
I. Me throughout the day looking for new catches.
J. The insides of a peeled trap reveal an assassin bug.
K. White flowers form at the end of a towering stalk to keep pollinators from certain death below.
L. Seeds are ready to be removed from a pollinated flower.
M. Please keep your legs inside the trap at all times.

B

D

E

F

H

I

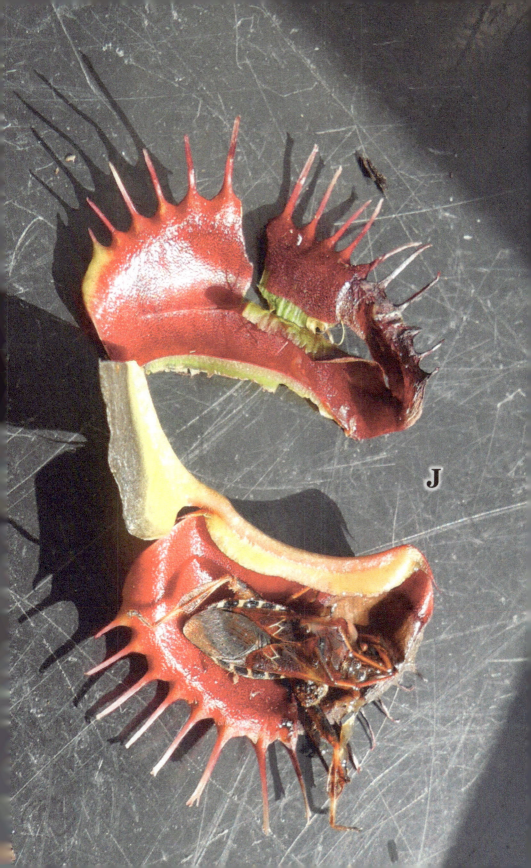

J

M

PITCHER PLANTS

Pitcher's tender throat,
Luring insects to their fall,
Nature's cunning trap.

OVERVIEW

Pitcher plants are probably the second most common commercially available carnivorous plant, and they look fantastic in any collection. There are many species all over the world, from temperate North American Pitchers (*Sarracenia*) to tropical pitchers (*Nepenthes*). They come in many brilliant colors with intricate leaf patterns. They are also easy to grow.

   All pitcher plants work the same. Insects are lured to the top portions of the pitchers where they feast on the nectar secreted around the rim and hood. It supposedly makes the insect a bit drunk. Downward pointing hairs and a waxy coating on the inside of the pitcher eventually cause the hapless prey to fall into a pool of water and digestive enzymes.

A LIFE WITH CARNIVOROUS PLANTS

Because of the numerous pitchers that can grow on a single plant in a season—over a dozen or more—and the size of the pitchers, these plants are voracious eaters. A single pitcher can be the final resting spot for hundreds of insects. My *Sarracenia* 'Judith Hindle' pitchers have an affinity for wasps, flies, and ants.

New pitchers form all season.

Insects pile up at the bottom.

It's very entertaining watching insects attempting to avoid the "pitfall" of the trap while maneuvering around. I've witnessed wasps straddling the rim with one or more legs bent over the sides as they sip away on the inner portions. Others are not so clever. They land and fall in within a minute. You'd think they could just fly out. But the farther they fall the waxier the wall sides become, and so it turns into a futile struggle of climbing and falling back down. New pitchers rapidly shoot up with the added nutrition.

PITCHER PLANTS

Nectar secretions around the rim and hood lure prey in.

This tropical *Nepenthes* 'Gaya' hybrid forms pitchers that hang from the tips of its leaves. It is also a wasp magnet.

A LIFE WITH CARNIVOROUS PLANTS

GROWING

Like the Venus flytrap, most pitchers plants love and need to be in full sun. The exceptions are the preceding *Nepenthes* variety that prefers mostly bright indirect light. This makes it suitable for indoor growing. The care of a pitcher plant depends on its native climate. Some are temperate and need dormancy, like the *Sarracenias*, and others thrive year-round, like *Nepenthes*. Here are some growing tips:

1. Pitchers plants should always remain moist, especially if grown outdoors. *Sarracenias* are perfect bog plants that you can grow outdoors in a tub with no drainage. They drink *a lot* of water. If you have a plant in a saucer, make sure it is a deep saucer as you may find yourself adding distilled or rainwater daily during the hot summer months. *Never* let them dry out.
2. *Sarracenias* enjoy full sun for 8 hours or more. Acclimate newly purchased plants from bright shade to full sun over a few weeks so the leaves don't burn. Again, *Nepenthes* do best in bright light (not full sun) only.
3. *Sarracenias* require a winter dormancy, just like the Venus flytrap. They pair well in bog gardens or planters. *Nepenthes* and other tropical pitchers plants do not require dormancy and should be brought inside during the cold winters. I keep mine a few feet from a southwest-facing window in the kitchen with a humidifier running when the humidity drops below 50%.
4. I grow all my pitchers in the same carnivorous plant mix of three parts peat moss to one part perlite. A bit of horticultural sand may be used with *Sarracenias*. Just make sure it is not beach sand, which can contain salts and other minerals. *Nepenthes* like a more open mix with sphagnum moss. Some growers prefer only sphagnum.

PITCHER PLANTS

Pitcher plants can quickly fill out their pots. The best time to repot is just before they come out of dormancy. This one I did mid-summer from an unexpected growth spurt.

Here is this original *Sarracenia purpurea* as purchased.

Rescued from a nursery checkout counter.

A LIFE WITH CARNIVOROUS PLANTS

FEEDING

As with Venus flytraps, let mother nature run its course. You don't have to place bugs into the pitchers if they are growing outside. I have a fourth-floor balcony where wasps, ants, flies, spiders, stink bugs, assassin bugs, and more seem to find their way. Pitchers will feast on anything that falls in.

You may notice that some pitchers have hoods that prevent too much rain from getting in. They excrete a cocktail of water and enzymes into the pitchers on their own. Others have open hoods, like this *Sarracenia purpurea*. This allows rain to fill the pitcher for its specific needs. It's okay to squirt some distilled or rainwater into these from time to time.

PITCHER PLANTS

If you are growing a *Nepenthes* indoors, you can also drop a few dead insects inside. Mealworms from the pet store are also a nutritious treat.

DORMANCY

Sarracenia dormancy requirements are the same as those for Venus flytraps, which is why I group them together inside my outdoor cold shelter. I only cut off completely dead pitchers until spring. With Virginia winter temperature fluctuations, I've seen flies take to the tubes as late as December.

Tubes that have not turned brown also provide energy for the plant through photosynthesis.

When spring rolls around, I will carefully cut off all of last season's pitchers without nipping any new growth or flowers. Take your time when you do this. *Sarracenia* will shoot up new leaves as early as February in many locations throughout the Southeast.

This is a good time to slice open a few dead pitchers to see what the traps captured the previous season. You'll be amazed at the hundreds of bugs it consumed.

My *Nepenthes* return inside and hang in front of the window in the winter until outdoor nighttime temperatures exceed 50 degrees. This is usually mid-May in Virginia.

Nepenthes placed in a plant hanger with a saucer.

PITCHER PLANTS

PROPAGATING

There are several ways to propagate your pitcher plants, and the best methods depend on the species. *Sarracenia*s divide easily. *Nepenthes* pitchers propagate well with cuttings. Here are the easiest methods, in my opinion.

Division

After a few years of growing this *Sarracenia* 'Judith Hindle', you can see that several groupings have formed.

First purchased in May 2021.

How it looked in July 2023.

In the late winter/early spring, just before the plants begin to come out of dormancy, you can separate your *Sarracenia*. It's best to cut off all the dead pitchers so you can easily see the growth. Be careful not to cut the tips of new growth or flowers that may already be shooting up from the base. This particular plant is showing natural groupings from its rhizomes where I will want to wiggle back and forth and break off. If you can't easily spot separation points, wash off the soil with distilled or rainwater. Repot plants separately.

Seeds

You can easily pollinate a single pitcher plant with itself or others. To do so on a *Sarracenia* pitcher plant, you will need to know the basic flower parts. Below is a ripe flower where pollen is forming on the tips of the stamens (known as anthers). That pollen will collect in the upside-down umbrella part of the flower. With a small paint brush, collect some pollen on the tip of the brush. Next, pull down the star-point stigmas of the same or another flower of a different plant and apply the pollen to the insides of the tips. You will see the small stigma nubs. Do all five stigmas of the flower.

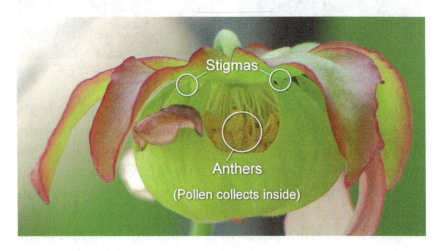

PITCHER PLANTS

If a flower is successfully pollinated, it will eventually form a large ovary in the top underside. You'll want to wait till late fall before you harvest any seeds. The ovary will turn brown and sometimes crack open. Be patient.

A nearly ripened ovary about to crack open in the fall.

Harvesting dozens of seeds from inside the ovary.

Once you have seeds, you can store them in the fridge dry, or do what is called stratification. This is a necessary step to ensure proper germination. Place the seeds between two paper towels and mist till damp. Cover and put that in the refrigerator or wherever you can achieve temperatures around 40 degrees Fahrenheit. Make sure you label the container with the species of seeds and place the date on top. Allow 6-8 weeks for the seeds to stratify. Open the cover once a week to check for mold and to allow for air change. Remove any moldy seeds or tissue if necessary.

Wetting the paper towels with a light spray mister of distilled water.

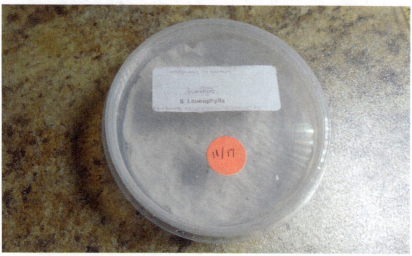
Sealing the container with species name and date on top.

PITCHER PLANTS

After the seeds have been properly stratified, you can place them on top of moist soil. I recommend sterilizing the dry peat moss mixture beforehand by baking at 200 degrees Fahrenheit for one hour. Do not bury the seeds. Provide bright light and a humidity dome. Keep them moist with occasional bottom watering as you would with a mature plant, but don't let the tray stay sitting in water until you see plants.

Yaungel Seed Starter Trays with humidity domes.

Sarracenia pitcher seeds germinating about a month later.

Hybridization

There are many hybrids of pitchers plants, meaning they have been cross-pollinated with other pitcher plants for different variations in leaf traits and colors. For instance, according to its registration with the ICPS (International Carnivorous Plant Society), my *Sarracenia* 'Judith Hindle' includes crosses between *Sarracenia leucophylla* and *Sarracenia flava rugelli* and *Sarracenia purpurea chipola*.

S. leucophylla   *S. flava*   *S. purpurea*

Sarracenia 'Judith Hindle'

Notice the characteristics and colors acquired from the crosses.

PITCHER PLANTS

Sarracenia 'Judith Hindle' pitchers in the mid-summer.

A LIFE WITH CARNIVOROUS PLANTS

Cuttings

Tropical pitcher plants like this *Nepenthes* 'Gaya' can be propagated with basal shoot or vine cuttings. Sometimes a plant will form offshoots known as basal plants. You will see them around the base of the mother plant with their own main stalk and pitchers.

Basal shoots rising from the soil and attached to the mother plant.

Remove some soil to see where the basal shoots are attached to the main plant. Once you do, you can take a pair of sterilized shears and carefully snip them off.

PITCHER PLANTS

Wrap the cut area and stem with wet sphagnum moss and plant them in a pot. Here, I surrounded the moss clump with a mixture of peat moss, perlite, and more sphagnum moss. Pre-moisten the soil with distilled water and wring it out before potting.

Set the basal plant pots in a tray of distilled water and provide bright light and high humidity. The plants should begin to root within a few weeks or so. Some leaves may die.

If you have a pitcher plant that grows a long vine without any pitchers, you can cut off the vine and separate it into pieces. Cut just below a leaf and leave one or two more leaves above. Remove the bottom leaf so you'll have a growth node to plant under the soil. Cut the other leaves in half to focus energy on root production. Pot the same as a basal shoot.

A LIFE WITH CARNIVOROUS PLANTS

GALLERY

A. The downward-pointing hairs of a *Sarracenia purpurea*.
B. Every year a line of ants crosses over my balcony. This *Sarracenia purpurea* quickly snatches them up.
C. A *Sarracenia* 'Judith Hindle' gobbles up more ants.
D. *Sarracenia* catches the summer evening sunlight.
E. The magnificent, red-veined pattern with hints of pink on a maturing *Sarracenia* 'Judith Hindle' leaf.
F. *Nepenthes* 'Gaya' pitchers grow larger after consuming lots of prey.
G. Top: Yellowjackets accumulate at the bottom of a *Nepenthes* 'Gaya'. Bottom: The digested remains of several unfortunate victims.
H. A fly becomes an unwary victim of a *Sarracenia* pitcher.
I. A *Sarracenia* pitcher plant awakens from dormancy.
J. In spring a green *Sarracenia* 'Judith Hindle' leaf and a new flower emerge.
K. A month later the flower turned red and is opening to accept pollinators.
L. At the end of winter, I remove a few of the dead pitcher leaves and split them open to check for catches.
M. Hundreds of leftover bug parts spill out.
N. A yellowjacket and a small fly in a *Sarracenia purpurea*.

B

E

F

G

J

K

SUNDEWS

Sundew's sticky threads,
Crimson drops on emerald bed,
Insects meet their end.

OVERVIEW

Sundews are the sparkling jewels of the carnivorous plant world. That's how they received their common name—the sun glistening off the dew-like droplets at the tips of their tentacle-like structures. What wouldn't be attracted to that? But beware! This is not a place any insect wants to be.

Sundews lure their victims with both the red color and nectar-promising leaves. But that nectar is like glue. Once prey lands on it, a futile struggle ensues with more tentacles bending toward the victim until they are encased in a mucilaginous trap. And in many sundew species, the entire leaf will curl around the victim's body. After the insects are digested and absorbed back into the plant, the tentacles will unfurl and wait for another meal.

A LIFE WITH CARNIVOROUS PLANTS

GROWING

There are tropical and temperate sundews, so some require a winter dormancy. Most require bright to full sunlight. However, in my experience, they are not as fond of high temperatures as Venus flytraps or pitcher plants. If you live in an area where temperatures often exceed 100 degrees Fahrenheit, I'd suggest keeping them in a slightly cooler but sunny location. Here are common growing conditions for most commercially available sundews.

1. Pot them in a carnivorous plant soil mixture of peat moss and perlite.
2. Kept them moist at all times by sitting in distilled water.
3. Provide high humidity, but do not mist them. This is true for all carnivorous plants.
4. Bright outdoor sun with a bit of filtration suits them well. In a bog garden, taller pitcher plants help provide a bit of shade relief throughout the day. Sundews make excellent bog and terrarium plants.

Sundews in a tray help rid this adjacent houseplant of its pesky gnats.

SUNDEWS

Drosera filiformis sundews have thread-like leaves.

There are nearly 200 species of *Drosera* sundew plants throughout the world. In this chapter, I will discuss care for the tropical *Drosera capensis*, also known as the Cape Sundew, and the temperate *Drosera filiformis*.

Because I have a southwest-facing balcony that gets quite hot during the summer, I keep my *Drosera capensis* plants under grow lights inside. They do best sitting in a tray of distilled water with a clear, ventilated dome.

A LIFE WITH CARNIVOROUS PLANTS

On days when the temperature does not exceed 90 degrees Fahrenheit, I will remove the dome and place the tray outdoors in a bright area with indirect sunlight so they can feed on gnats and other small insects.

People will often ask why their sundews lack the dew on their leaves. Bright light, water, and humidity are what trigger the production of these telltale secretions, so make sure you are providing ample amounts of each. A new plant may also take time to acclimate to its new living situation.

For my *Drosera filiformis* plants, I place them in saucers or trays under my pitcher plants and Venus flytraps. This not only provides them with a bit of shade throughout the day, but it also protects them from heavy rain, which can wash off the dew or break down the leaves. For many species of *Drosera*, one doesn't need to be so overprotective. They can withstand full sun and plenty of heat. Some balconies, especially on higher floors, can trap a lot of heat and cause plants to bake during certain times of the year. Find out what gives you the best results for your location and species.

Drosera capensis and *filiformis* receive protection under other plants.

FEEDING

Though not as fast as a Venus flytrap, most sundews have the satisfying feature of moving their tentacles to trap prey. Through time-lapse photography, I've captured a *Drosera capensis* leaf completely rolling around a fly in just 24 minutes. The struggling of the prey is what accelerates the process, just as the continued movement of an insect within a flytrap expedites the leaf's full closure.

As with flytraps and pitcher plants, nature knows best. There is no shortage of small flying insects outdoors, like the kind that buzz around your head in swarms while you hike through the woods. If you keep your sundews indoors under grow lights, they are also the ultimate gnat eliminators. Fruit flies? No problem. They can wipe out a colony in just a few days. I've come to appreciate gnats and fruit flies and always try to find ways to guide them to my sundews.

Young *Drosera capensis* going to town on gnats.

A LIFE WITH CARNIVOROUS PLANTS

If you are short of gnats or fruit flies and growing your sundews inside a container that can be closed, you can create a temporary bug breeder by placing part of a ripened banana inside a plastic cup. Here, I sank half a ripe banana into a wine cup and placed it outdoors for two days. Once I noticed enough critters inside (more will hatch from eggs deposited inside the banana), I concealed the top with a plastic cover. After placing the cup inside my *Drosera capensis* tray, I knocked the top off and closed the dome vents. Let the feeding frenzy begin! All were captured by morning.

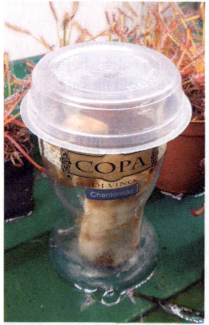
Dozens of fruit flies released.

Fruit fly gets sticky embrace.

You can also feed your sundews pieces of freeze-dried bloodworms, especially in the winter months when live insects are hard to find. Moisten them slightly first, then place them on the tentacles with a toothpick. Once a month will do. Bloodworms are available at your local pet store.

SUNDEWS

DORMANCY

As summer comes to an end and temperatures cool, the tropical sundews will return indoors. The temperate sundews will be placed inside my cold shelter all winter where the leaves will die back to form hibernaculum buds. It will appear as if the plant has completely died, but don't you worry. This is where new growth will begin in the spring.

Drosera filiformis sundews coming out of dormancy.

PROPAGATING

When provided with ample light, sundews flower often and easily multiply by dispersing hundreds of their seeds. Sundews are capable of self-pollinating. Some call *Drosera capensis* a weed because of that, but I absolutely love and treasure this easy-to-grow carnivore. Therefore, I suggest sowing seeds as the easiest method of propagation.

A LIFE WITH CARNIVOROUS PLANTS

Seeds

Drosera seeds are very tiny and can be harvested when the flowers turn brown. Sprinkle the seeds on top of your moistened carnivorous soil mix and keep them misted with distilled or rainwater. You don't need to stratify them. It takes about 4-6 weeks for *Drosera capensis* seeds to germinate. Give them plenty of light. Grow lights are best.

Four months later and the leaves have elongated.

SUNDEWS

Division

Some sundews will naturally propagate by sending out offshoots or "pups" at the base of the mother plant. Some will form tubers that can be separated. Research your *Drosera* species to see which is the most reliable method.

Cuttings

Finally, you can also increase many *Drosera* populations through leaf cuttings. Cut a few of the best leaves from multiple plants, float them on ¼" of distilled water in a clear container, and cover. Provide them with ample light, but don't place in full sun. Again, grow lights about 8-12" away do best. It may take a month or more for you to see little plantlets forming along the leaves. Once these plantlets are about 1/2" wide, you can carefully plant them in a moist peat moss mixture and cover with a ventilated humidity dome.

Drosera capensis leaf cuttings.

Babies forming 6 weeks later.

A LIFE WITH CARNIVOROUS PLANTS

GALLERY

A. The maturing leaves of a *Drosera capensis*.
B. A blue damselfly trapped in multiple leaves.
C. Leaf curls around a fly on a *Drosera capensis* leaf.
D. Several *Drosera capensis* plants gathered together.
E. Tentacles around a fruit fly on a *Drosera capensis* leaf.
F. The pink flowers of a *Drosera filiformis*.
G. Globules of dew trap a gnat on a *Drosera filiformis*.

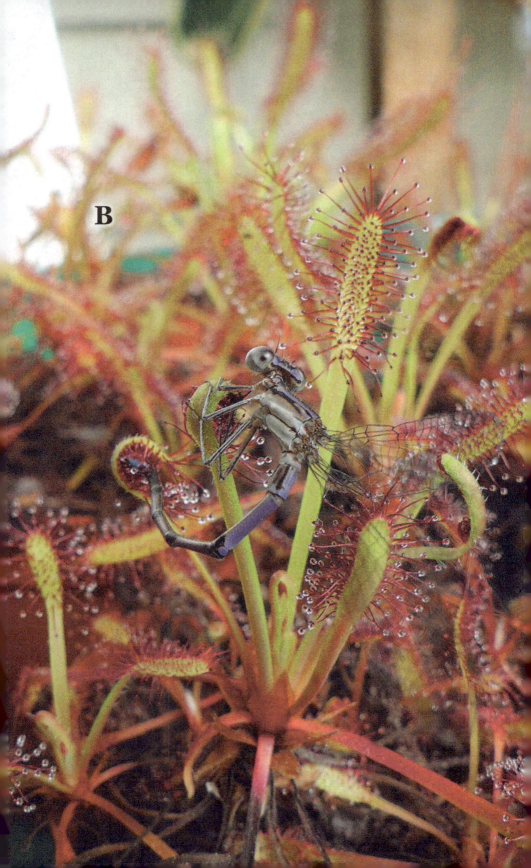

BUTTERWORTS

Butterworts glisten,
Trapping with a dewy kiss,
Prey caught in their woe.

OVERVIEW

There are over 80 species of butterworts (*Pinguicula*), and they can be found on almost every continent. Most come from Central and South America. We refer to those tropical varieties as Mexican butterworts. There are also temperate and warm temperate species, like *Pinguicula primuliflora*, which has its native habitat in the southeastern United States.

    Butterworts have oval or oblong-shaped leaves that form a rosette. The leaves are covered with tiny, sticky hairs that attract insects searching for water or nectar. Small insects like gnats quickly become trapped in the mucilage and are easily digested and absorbed by the plant. Sometimes the edges of the leaves will curl inward to prevent the digestive enzymes from flowing over.

A LIFE WITH CARNIVOROUS PLANTS

Butterworts (*Pinguicula*) are nature's efficient gnat removers.

Butterworts are also known for their long and colorful flower stalks.

BUTTERWORTS

GROWING

Butterworts prefer bright light and moist soil during the growing season. Peat moss with perlite and sand mixed in makes an excellent growing medium. Warm temperate butterworts, like the *Pinguicula primuliflora*, thrive in wet soil, whereas Mexican butterworts grow best in moist and rocky (extra perlite) soil that has good drainage. During dormancy, they should be watered less frequently, but the soil should remain mostly damp. Though some species may have more detailed requirements, here are a few general rules for keeping your butterworts thriving:

1. Bright sun is okay, but too much can burn the leaves. They make great indoor windowsill plants as long as the sun isn't too intense, so I recommend keeping them a foot or more away from south-facing windows.
2. If grown indoors under grow lights, keep them about a foot away from the lights or not directly under them. Start out farther away for a week or so and gradually add more light. Bright light will bring out the pink or purple color pigments in some of the species. Too much light will turn the leaves brown.
3. Again, use only distilled or rainwater and water from the bottom.
4. Pay attention to the dormancy requirements for each species as they can vary. More in the Dormancy section.

Many growers will place warm temperate butterworts in outdoor container gardens with pitcher plants and Venus flytraps to shade them from the hot midday sun. I prefer to keep mine under indoor grow lights during the winter, and outdoors in bright shade during the summer so they can feed on gnats, mosquitoes, and other small flying pests.

Trays of potted butterworts under a grow light.

A small *Pinguicula* rock garden with three different species.

Butterworts come in various colors as well. Add a bit more light to reveal their true colors in nature. Take a look at the following *Pinguicula* 'Pirouette' after growing for a few months a bit closer to the grow lights.

BUTTERWORTS

The leaves begin to reveal their pinkish hues with added light.

A very deep red *Pinguicula planifolia* in the wild.

One notable observation about butterworts is that they don't have a vast root system. They develop just enough roots to attach themselves to the substrate and take up water. This makes them easy to repot. Be careful not to break off the grow point in the center or get soil on the leaves. If you accidentally remove a leaf, you can propagate it. See the Propagating section in this chapter.

A LIFE WITH CARNIVOROUS PLANTS

Butterworts often ship bareroot in closed containers for protection.

FEEDING

Butterworts are God's answer to those nasty and prolific gnats that thrive in the fertile soil of common houseplants. Gnats are drawn to butterworts like...gnat paper. But mosquitoes, fruit flies, and other small pests can also fall victim to the sticky leaves. They are great for a kitchen windowsill.

BUTTERWORTS

If you notice that your indoor butterworts are not catching any bugs and the leaves are sticky, you can mix Shultz Cactus fertilizer with distilled water as per instructions and spray lightly once directly onto the leaves with a mist bottle. Do this about once a month. If your plants are outdoors, only do this around dusk or early morning so the water does not cause leaf burn under bright sun. Preferably, outdoor butterworts will catch lots of insects and you won't need to mist on any fertilizer.

DORMANCY

Mexican or tropical butterworts may enter a "succulent" hibernation stage if the temperatures are a bit cooler and daylight length shortens. This is normal. The leaves will appear as small rosettes and will not be active traps. You don't have to do anything different but water a bit less. They can become almost dry, but not completely dry. Within a few months or so they will form new trap leaves again.

Every butterwort is a bit different. One may go into hibernation while the one next to it does not. Just let it take the lead. If in the spring it is not coming out of dormancy, slowly add a bit more light, or water it a bit more. Subtle changes will trigger the return to a carnivorous state.

A Mexican butterwort that has entered a hibernation stage.

Warm temperate butterworts from the southeastern states will stay green during the winter months but slow in growth. However, I have had great success with my *Pinguicula primuliflora* under indoor grow lights year-round. Cold temperate or "hardy" butterworts can die back into hibernacula till spring. Check online for each species that you obtain for specific requirements.

PROPAGATING

Butterworts can be best propagated through seeds and leaf pulls. Some, like the *Pinguicula primuliflora,* will even form babies where the leaf tips touch the soil.

BUTTERWORTS

Seeds

To pollinate a flower, blacken the end of a toothpick with a marker. Stick it into a flower and push up the stigma to access the anthers behind. Press up to get some yellow pollen stuck onto the toothpick. Rub the pollen onto the stigma of a flower of a different plant that is not an offspring.

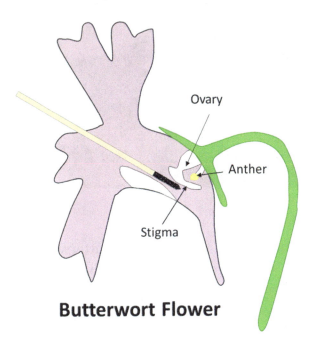

Butterwort Flower

A LIFE WITH CARNIVOROUS PLANTS

Seeds will ripen within a month after successful pollination. Only cold temperate butterwort seeds need 8-12 weeks of stratification. Others you can plant right away. You should notice germination within 1-2 months.

Division

Some butterworts will form multiple plants around each other, and if they do, you can easily separate the rosettes by removing the entire clump from the soil and gently rocking them free at the soil line. Repot separately.

Cuttings

The easiest method to propagate butterworts is through leave pulls. Gently rock a lower leaf back and forth while holding the plant in place so you don't pull it out of the soil. Remember not to damage the crown of the plant. The leaf should pull and have a white end. That is where the plantlets

BUTTERWORTS

will form. Place leaves on a damp paper towel or damp sphagnum with the tip touching or slightly under the medium or a towel crease. Cover for humidity and provide bright light. New plants should form in a month or so.

Small plantlet forming at the tip of the leaf after six weeks.

A LIFE WITH CARNIVOROUS PLANTS

GALLERY

A. An ant trapped on the dewy leaf of *Pinguicula vulgaris*.
B. The colorful hues of a Mexican butterwort.
C. Mexican butterwort with purple leaf edges.
D. The trap and succulent stages of a *Pinguicula*.
E. A sea of flowers from *Pinguicula emarginata*.
F. A tiny *Pinguicula debbertiana* rests on a mossy carpet.

E

A LIFE WITH CARNIVOROUS PLANTS

MORE TO EXPLORE!

There are hundreds of species of carnivorous plants.

Darlingtonia californica

Nepenthes aristolochioides

Dionaea muscipula 'Bristle Tooth'

Drosera adelae

CONCLUSION

Before you go, I'd like to talk about planning for the future of your *own* carnivorous plant life. How many plants do you want to have? Will you be able to take care of them all? When does it become an obsession and no longer a hobby?

There is no doubt that owning and growing carnivorous plants is addictive. There are so many species and colors and shapes and sizes. It's amazing that nature has produced such wonderful specimens.

I began my collection with two Venus flytraps from big box stores, two pitcher plants from a nursery, and seeds from another. Along the way I added a few butterwort species that I ordered online. From there I just propagated what I had to my heart's content. Well, then I bought more seeds.

You may want to grow and sell carnivorous plants as a side or full-time business. Or, you may just want to expand your collection a little bit at a time. Whatever you do, make sure it's right for you and the time you can put into it.

Understand that these plants have very special needs, unlike your typical houseplants. Carnivorous plants require a lot of water. Letting them dry out can kill many of the plants quite quickly. That means you will have to check on them often—even daily—during the hot summer months. And you have to distinguish between which plants require dormancy, and which do not. But once you figure it out and come up with a yearly routine, it all gets a lot simpler.

Expanding part of my collection with a shelf, trays, and winter cover.

This book was designed to get you started on a path to successfully growing and maintaining a healthy carnivorous plant collection. There is no doubt that there are advanced hobbyists and professional growers whose knowledge and experience goes well beyond the scope of what is covered here. There is also information out there that is contradictory to standard practices. For example, some may say to stratify seeds for 6 weeks, whereas someone else will say 2-3 months. Seek out online forums for consensus and experienced growers for more "tried-and-true" knowledge. Even *they* learn new things every day.

CONCLUSION

A lucky fly waits for the trap to reopen so it can escape.

VIDEOS

Check out my carnivorous plant videos on YouTube, as well as other channels listed in the Resources chapter. Though I don't provide instructions, mine are more of the "plants in action" type. My pitcher plants are voracious yellowjacket eaters, and it's not uncommon to catch on video a new yellowjacket making a tragic pitfall once an hour in the late fall. The URL is http://youtube.com/@VictorRook/playlists.

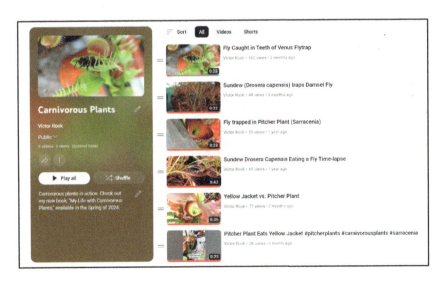

A LIFE WITH CARNIVOROUS PLANTS

Set up your own camera for live and time-lapse videos. Many cameras have time-lapse functions where you can set the interval on when each picture is taken. You never know what you'll "capture" in the wild world of carnivorous plants.

Filming a time-lapse video of a Venus flytrap leaf sealing up.

YOUR SUPPORT

I hope this book was helpful to you. I hope that you found useful information that will get you started on your carnivorous plant journey. If it was helpful, please take the time to write a review on Amazon. I appreciate your support and kind words. It was a joy putting this book together. Vic

RESOURCES

PLANT SUPPLIERS

Visit these websites to order plants and supplies or visit their locations if they are open to the public.

California Carnivores (California)
https://www.californiacarnivores.com/

Predatory Plants (California)
https://predatoryplants.com/

Carnivorous Plant Nursery (Maryland)
https://carnivorousplantnursery.com/

Blue Ridge Exotics (North Carolina)
https://www.blueridgeexotics.com/

Curious Plant Carnivorous Plant Nursery (Ohio)
https://curiousplant.com/

Sarracenia Northwest (Oregon)
https://www.growcarnivorousplants.com/

A LIFE WITH CARNIVOROUS PLANTS

Redleaf Exotics (Tennessee)
https://redleafexotics.com/

PetFlyTrap (Texas)
https://www.petflytrap.com/

Carnivero (Texas)
https://www.carnivero.com/

Triffid Park (Australia)
https://www.triffidpark.com.au/

Carnivorous Plant Store (Canada)
https://www.carnivorousplantstore.com/

Hampshire Carnivorous Plants (UK)
https://www.hantsflytrap.com/

LIGHTING & MORE

Here are links to the products I've mentioned and use for my collection. These affiliate links help support my efforts.

SZHLUX Grow Light (2 x 40W)
https://amzn.to/49SturJ

Carnivorous Plant Soil
https://amzn.to/3sNGVbJ. Also check Plant Suppliers.

Shinegro Mini Greenhouse (19" x 19" x 15")
https://amzn.to/40WevZC

Gardzen Plant Trays
https://amzn.to/3SYt516

RESOURCES

Yaungel Seed Starter Trays with Humidity Domes
https://amzn.to/47znWRC

LeJoy Growing Tray Mini Greenhouse
https://amzn.to/3sHmn4S

Topeakmart 2-Tier Metal Plant Stand
https://amzn.to/3sFXTJf

Gardzen Greenhouse Cover for Plant Stand
https://amzn.to/47u9IkT

Schultz Cactus Plus Liquid Plant Food (Use on Butterworts)
https://amzn.to/4aaxAMb

BioAdvanced 3-in-1 Insect, Disease, & Mite Control
https://www.amazon.com/dp/B000RUJZS6

Bionide Systemic Insect Control
https://amzn.to/3GnW5YB

SOCIAL MEDIA

Learn and share with other carnivorous plant enthusiasts.

Facebook Groups

Beginner Carnivorous Plant Growers
https://www.facebook.com/groups/810711769793222

Carnivorous Plant Resource Group
https://www.facebook.com/groups/777169342453509

Carnivorous Plants Community
https://www.facebook.com/groups/263987903694872

A LIFE WITH CARNIVOROUS PLANTS

International Carnivorous Plant Society Forum
https://www.facebook.com/groups/1454798608087049

Venus Fly Trap Enthusiasts
https://www.facebook.com/groups/2468060651

Nepenthes Only
https://www.facebook.com/groups/628807417640850

Carnivorous Plants Marketplace
https://www.facebook.com/groups/1109523769234584

YouTube Channels

youtube.com/@California_Carnivores
youtube.com/@SarraceniaNorthwest
youtube.com/@redleafexotics4722
youtube.com/@CarnivorousPlantsHub
youtube.com/@carnivorousplantsjourney1940
youtube.com/@TheFlytrapGarden
youtube.com/@venusflytrapworld
youtube.com/@mypingtopia
youtube.com/@WindowsillNepenthes
youtube.com/@PredatoryPlants

Instagram

https://www.instagram.com/carnivorousplant_club
https://www.instagram.com/carnivorousplantresource
https://www.instagram.com/hampshirecarnivorousplants
https://www.instagram.com/jeremiahsplants

Made in the USA
Las Vegas, NV
05 April 2024

88293759R00085